Merry Christmas Sis,
Thought you might
enjoy this for use
when Market day
comes around again

Love

Dagmar

1998

Design: Jill Coote
Recipe Photography: Peter Barry
Jacket and Illustration Artwork: Jane Winton,
courtesy of Bernard Thornton Artists, London
Editors: Jillian Stewart, Kate Cranshaw and Laura Potts

CLB 3515
Published by Grange Books,
an imprint of Grange Books PLC,
The Grange, Grange Yard, London.
© 1994 CLB Publishing,
Godalming, Surrey, England.
All rights reserved.
Printed and bound in Singapore
Published 1994
ISBN 1-85627-424-1

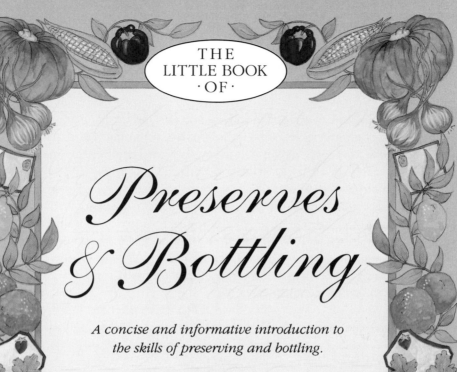

THE LITTLE BOOK · OF ·

Preserves & Bottling

A concise and informative introduction to the skills of preserving and bottling.

Grange
BOOKS

Introduction

$\mathcal{T}$ he skills of preserving and bottling are fast becoming one of the forgotten arts of cookery, with people preferring the ease and convenience of buying the mass-produced, commercial product available in shops to making their own. Yet, when home-made preserves or pickles are available on a produce stall at a fair or sale, their quality and flavour ensures they are among the very first items to be sold. Though making jams and pickles needs both time and patience, it is well worth the effort, with the finished result being far superior to commercial products. In addition, it is an ideal way of making use of the glut of cheap fruit and vegetables that are available in the summer and early autumn.

Preserves can roughly be divided into three categories, jellies, jams and marmalades. Jellies are made from the strained juice of puréed fruit, while jams are made from whole, cut or pulped fruits, and marmalades from small, thin slices of citrus fruit. In each case the fruit is combined with sugar and water and heated until the setting point is reached. Testing for this set can be done in a number of ways. The most popular is to spoon a small amount of the liquid onto a plate, where it should cool quickly and wrinkle when pushed with the finger.

Pectin, the substance that makes jams, jellies and marmalades set, is vital to the process of making preserves. It is found naturally in fruits, with the greatest quantities occurring in the skin, seeds and core. Some fruits contain much greater quantities of pectin than others, particularly apples, blackcurrants, plums and citrus fruits. In the past, small quantities of these fruits were used when making preserves with fruits that were low in pectin such as cherries, strawberries, raspberries, blackberries and rhubarb, to ensure that they set. The development of commercial pectin has, save for the purposes of flavour, made this technique obsolete. Among the most popular forms in which to buy pectin, and probably the easiest to use, is sugar jam, which combines granulated sugar and powdered pectin. It is important to follow recipes carefully to minimise the risk of problems in getting the preserve to set.

Pickling produce works on a slightly different principal to preserving. Preserves are made by using sugar to neutralise the affects of bacteria in fresh produce by dehydrating them, while pickles use acid, in most cases vinegar, to curtail the growth of unwanted bacteria, so stopping the food from going off. When pickling it is important to use produce that is at the very peak of condition and to prepare it carefully as just one damaged vegetable can spoil the produce in a whole container.

The selection of recipes in this book provide the perfect introduction to the age-old skills of preserving and bottling, allowing you to discover the truly unique flavour of traditional, home-made preserves and pickles. With clear, step-by-step instructions and a host of useful tips, it guides you through some of the main techniques, as well as principles underlying them, helping to get perfect results every time.

Whole Strawberry Conserve with Grand Marnier

MAKES About 2.7kg/6lbs

This luxury preserve will make an attractive gift for a 'foodie' friend or relative. Make sure that you use only firm, unblemished berries.

PREPARATION: 10 mins
COOKING: 10 mins

1.8kg/4lbs strawberries
1.8kg/4lbs preserving sugar with added pectin
60ml/4 tbsps lemon juice
60ml/4 tbsps Grand Marnier

1. Hull the strawberries, wash them and leave to dry.

2. Layer the strawberries into a preserving pan, sprinkling the sugar between each layer.

3. Set aside until the juice begins to run.

4. Heat gently, stirring carefully until the sugar has dissolved. Add the lemon juice, then boil rapidly for 5 minutes.

5. Remove from the heat and test for the set, some spooned onto a cold plate and left for 2 minutes should wrinkle when tilted. If necessary boil for a few more minutes.

6. Stir in the Grand Marnier. Allow the jam to cool considerably then stir to distribute the strawberries and pot into warm, sterilized jars. Seal and label.

Paradise Jam

MAKES About 1.8kg/4lbs

This jam is made from a selection of exotic fruits, now readily available in most supermarkets.

PREPARATION: 15 mins
COOKING: 40 mins

---

2 large pawpaw (papaya)
4 passion fruit
2 guava
340g/12oz canned crushed pineapple, in
    natural juice
About 140ml/¼ pint water
2 tbsps lime juice
1.4kg/3lbs preserving sugar with added pectin

1. Peel and finely chop the pawpaw, and place in a preserving pan.

2. Cut the passion fruit in half, scoop out pulp and seeds, then add to the pan.

3. Peel and chop the guava and add to the pan.

4. Drain the pineapple and make juice up to 250ml/9 fl oz with water.

5. Add to the pan along with the pineapple.

6. Stir in the lime juice and cook gently until the fruit is very soft and pulpy.

7. Stir in the sugar, then heat gently, stirring until the sugar is dissolved.

8. Boil rapidly until setting point is reached. Some spooned onto a cold plate and left for 2 minutes should wrinkle when tilted.

9. Pour into hot, sterilized jars, then seal and label.

Rhubarb and Raspberry Jam

MAKES About 2kg/4½lbs

Raspberries can be expensive but when mixed with rhubarb which is both cheap and plentiful when in season, just a few will produce a delicious fruity jam.

PREPARATION: 30 mins
COOKING: 40 mins

680g/1½lbs rhubarb, cut into small pieces
140ml/¼ pint water
680g/1½lbs raspberries
3 tbsps lemon juice
1.4kg/3lbs granulated sugar

1. Place the rhubarb with the water, in a preserving pan and simmer gently for 10 minutes or until the rhubarb is just soft.

2. Add the raspberries and lemon juice and continue to cook for 10 minutes or until all the fruit is very soft.

3. Stir in the sugar and cook gently stirring

Cut the rhubarb into even-sized pieces about 1.25cm/½-inch long.

until all the sugar has dissolved.

4. Boil rapidly until setting point is reached; some spooned onto a cold plate and left for 2 minutes should wrinkle when tilted.

5. Allow to stand for 20 minutes then stir. Pour into hot, sterilized jars, seal and label.

Blueberry Jam with Cassis

MAKES About 1.8kg/4lbs

A sweet jam which can be made from fresh or frozen blueberries.

PREPARATION: 10 mins
COOKING: 35 mins

900g/2lbs blueberries
280ml/½ pint water
3 tbsps lemon juice
900g/2lbs sugar with added pectin
60ml/4 tbsps crème de cassis (blackcurrant
   liqueur)

---

1. Place the blueberries, water and lemon juice in a preserving pan, and cook until the fruit is very soft.

2. Stir in the sugar and cook gently, stirring until all the sugar has dissolved.

3. Boil rapidly for 5 minutes.

4. Remove from the heat and test for set; some spooned onto a cold plate and left for 2 minutes should wrinkle when tilted.

5. Boil for a little longer if required.

6. Stir in the crème de cassis.

7. Pour into hot, sterilized jars, then seal and label.

Lemon Lime Curd

MAKES About 680g/1½lbs

Delicious spread on bread or as a filling for cakes.

PREPARATION: 10 mins
COOKING: 50 mins

Grated rind and juice of 2 lemons
Grated rind and juice of 1 lime
45g/1½oz unsalted butter
225g/8oz caster sugar
3 eggs, beaten

1. Place the rind and juice of the fruit into the top of a double boiler or in a bowl placed over a pan of gently simmering water.

2. Add the butter and heat until melted. Stir in

Finely grate the rind of the lemons and lime.

Step 4 The curd is cooked when the mixture evenly coats the back of a wooden spoon.

the sugar and continue cooking until it has dissolved, stirring occasionally.

3. Strain the beaten eggs into the juice mixture and cook gently until the curd thickens, stirring constantly. Take care not to over heat the mixture or it will curdle. If the mixture does start to curdle remove from the heat immediately and whisk rapidly.

4. The curd is cooked when the mixture coats the back of a spoon.

5. Pour into dry, sterilized jars, seal and label. Store in the refrigerator until required.

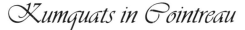

Kumquats in Cointreau

MAKES About 680g/1½lbs

Preserved whole fruits look and taste deliciously exotic. Serve with ice-cream or as part of a fruit salad.

PREPARATION: 15-20 mins
COOKING: 45 mins-1 hr

460g/1lb whole kumquats
225g/8oz granulated sugar
420ml/¾ pint water
3 tbsps Cointreau

---

1. Cut a cross in the top of each kumquat and pack into screw top heatproof preserving jars.

2. Heat the sugar and water gently until the sugar dissolves, then boil for 1 minute. Stir in the Cointreau.

3. Pour the syrup over the kumquats to within 1 cm/⅓ inch of the top of the jar. Screw the lids

Step 1 Pack the kumquats into heatproof glass preserving jars.

onto the jars then release a quarter turn.

4. Place several layers of folded newspaper in the bottom of a pan which is deep enough to fill with water to the top of the jars. Place the jars in the pan.

5. Fill the pan with water, up to the necks of the jars and heat slowly to simmering point – this should take about 30 minutes.

6. Maintain the water at simmering point for 10 minutes or until the kumquats look clear.

7. Remove the jars from the water and place on a wooden surface. Immediately fully tighten the lids and allow to cool completely.

8. Label and store in a cool dark place.

Step 1 Cut a small cross in the rounded end of each kumquat.

Ginger Pear Jam

MAKES About 2.3kg/5lbs

Often a glut of pears leaves you wondering how you can use them up. This recipe is an ideal way, allowing you to savour the taste of fresh pears right through the winter.

PREPARATION: 20 mins
COOKING: 50 mins

1.8kg/4lbs firm pears
850ml/1½ pints water
60g/2oz grated fresh root ginger
Juice of 1 lemon
1.4kg/3lbs granulated sugar

---

1. Peel and core the pears, and cut them into thick slices. Place in a preserving pan with the water, ginger and lemon juice.

Step 1 Cut the pears into thick slices with a sharp knife.

Step 2 Tie the peel, core and lemon skins in a square of muslin.

2. Tie the peel and core in a square of muslin, and add to the pan. Cook the pears for about 30 minutes, or until soft and pulpy.

3. Remove the muslin bag. Mash the fruit or push through a sieve.

4. Stir in the sugar and heat gently, stirring until it is dissolved.

5. Boil rapidly until the setting point is reached. This should take about 20 minutes. Draw a wooden spoon through the mixture, if the spoon leaves a channel setting point has been reached.

6. Pour into hot, sterilized jars, seal and label.

Kiwi Fruit and Apple Honey

MAKES About 1kg/2¼lbs

A refreshing and interesting preserve that spreads like honey.

PREPARATION: 15 mins
COOKING: 50 mins

---

4 kiwi fruit
140ml/¼ pint water
460g/1lb sugar
460g/1lb honey
400g/14oz cooking apples, peeled, cored and
   finely chopped
1 tsp lemon juice
Green food colouring (optional)

---

1. Peel and chop the kiwi fruit.

2. Heat the water, sugar and honey together in a preserving pan, stirring until all the sugar dissolves.

3. Add the kiwi fruit, apple and lemon juice and cook very gently until the preserve darkens and thickens.

4. Stir frequently to prevent the jam from burning.

5. Allow the jam to cool slightly, then place in a food processor and blend until smooth, adding a little green food colouring, if wished.

6. Leave to stand a few minutes to allow the bubbles to disperse, then pour into hot, sterilized jars. Seal and label.

Pineapple Grapefruit Marmalade

MAKES About 2.3kg/5lbs

The flavours of pineapple and grapefruit complement each other wonderfully as demonstrated in this delicious and unusual recipe.

PREPARATION: 1 hr
COOKING: 1½ hrs

2 large pineapples
3 grapefruit
570ml/1 pint water
680g/1½lbs granulated sugar
15g/½oz butter (if necessary)

1. Peel and cut the pineapples into small pieces.

2. Wash the grapefruit and pare off the zest with a sharp knife, taking care not to include too much of the white pith.

3. Cut the peel into shreds and squeeze the juice from the fruit.

4. Tie the remaining pith and seeds in a square of muslin.

Step 1 Peel the pineapple with a sharp knife.

Step 3 Cut the grapefruit peel into fine shreds.

5. Put the juice, peel, muslin bag and pineapple into a preserving pan with the water. Simmer gently for about 1 hour, or until the peel is soft.

6. Remove the muslin bag and squeeze out well. Stir in the sugar and heat gently, stirring until all the sugar is dissolved.

7. Boil rapidly without stirring until the setting point is reached. Some spooned onto a cold plate and left for 2 minutes should wrinkle when tilted.

8. If the marmalade looks bubbly and cloudy, stir the butter through the mixture to help clear it.

9. Allow to stand for 20 minutes before potting. Pour into hot, sterilized jars, seal and label.

Three Fruit Marmalade

MAKES About 1.6kg/3½lbs

This marmalade can be made at any time of the year, unlike those which include seville oranges in the ingredients.

PREPARATION: 45 mins
COOKING: 1½ hrs

4 limes
2 oranges
2 grapefruits
1.1 litres/2 pints water
900g/2lbs granulated sugar
30g/1oz butter (if necessary)

Step 2 Shred the citrus fruit zest into very thin strips.

1. Wash the fruit and pare off the zest with a sharp knife, taking care not to include too much of the white pith.

2. Cut the zest into shreds and squeeze the juice from the fruit.

3. Tie the remaining pith and seeds in a square of muslin.

4. Put the juice, peel and muslin bag into a preserving pan with the water and simmer gently for about 1 hour, or until the peel is soft and the contents of the pan have been reduced by about half.

5. Remove the muslin bag, and squeeze out well. Stir in the sugar and heat gently, stirring until all the sugar has dissolved.

6. Boil rapidly without stirring until setting point is reached. Some spooned onto a cold plate and left for 2 minutes should wrinkle when tilted.

7. If the marmalade looks bubbly and cloudy, stir the butter through the mixture to help clear it.

8. Allow to stand for 20 minutes before potting. Pour into hot, sterilized jars, seal and label.

Plums in Port

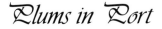

MAKES About 1.8kg/4lbs
This makes a very sophisticated dessert.

PREPARATION: 40 mins
COOKING: 40 mins

140ml/¼ pint water
225g/8oz sugar
280ml/½ pint ruby port
1.4kg/3lbs plums, halved and stoned
Few whole cloves

---

1. Heat the water and sugar, gently stirring until the sugar dissolves, then boil for a few minutes.

2. Remove from the heat and stir in the port.

3. Pack the plums into heatproof preserving jars and add 1 or 2 cloves to each jar.

4. Pour in the syrup to within 1cm/⅓ inch of the top of the jars. Add a little extra port if there is not enough syrup.

5. Screw the lids on then release a quarter turn.

6. Place several layers of folded newspaper in the bottom of a deep pan.

7. Put the jars in and fill the pan with water to the necks.

8. Heat slowly to simmering – this should take 30 minutes. Simmer for 10 minutes.

9. Turn off the heat, tighten the lids and allow the jars to cool completely in the water.

10. Label and store in a cool, dark place.

Pineapple, Mango and Mint Chutney

MAKES About 1.4kg/3lbs

This fresh tasting chutney makes an ideal accompaniment for curries, ploughman's lunches or cold pies.

PREPARATION: 20 mins
COOKING: 35 mins

1 large pineapple
Salt
2 large mangoes, peeled, stoned and chopped
225g/8oz sultanas
850ml/1½ pints distilled white vinegar
3 tbsps fresh mint, chopped
1 tbsp chopped fresh root ginger
½ tsp ground nutmeg
460g/1lb granulated sugar

1. Peel the pineapple and chop the fleash. Layer in a shallow dish and sprinkle liberally with salt and leave for several hours, or overnight.

2. Rinse the pineapple and drain well.

3. Place the pineapple, mango, sultanas, vinegar, mint, ginger and nutmeg in a preserving pan and simmer gently for 10 minutes until the fruits are tender.

4. Stir in the sugar and heat gently until it dissolves, then boil rapidly until thickened, stirring frequently to prevent it from burning on the bottom of the pan.

5. Test by stirring with a wooden spoon – if the spoon leaves a channel then the mixture is ready.

6. Pour into hot, sterilized jars, seal and label.

Curried Fruit

MAKES About 1kg/2¼lbs

This pickle is very quick to make and goes particularly well with cold pork.

PREPARATION: 15 mins
COOKING: 15 mins

225g/8oz demerara sugar
140ml/¼ pint distilled malt vinegar
140ml/¼ pint water
4 whole cloves
2 tbsps mild curry powder
1 tsp coriander seeds
3 apples, peeled, cored and thickly sliced
175g/6oz pineapple chunks
90g/3oz raisins
6 apricots, pitted and halved

1. Place the sugar, vinegar, water, cloves, curry powder and coriander seeds in a large saucepan or preserving pan.

2. Heat gently, stirring until the sugar dissolves, then boil for 2 minutes.

3. Add the apples, pineapple and raisins and cook for 5 minutes.

4. Add the apricots and cook for another 3 minutes. The apple should look translucent.

5. Pour into hot, sterilized jars, then seal and label.

6. After opening store in the refrigerator.

Bread and Butter Pickle

MAKES About 1kg/2¼lbs

A simple, attractive pickle. Serve with fish or cold meats.

PREPARATION: 15 mins, plus several hours
standing time
COOKING: 10 mins

570g/1¼lbs pickling cucumbers
1 large onion
Salt
570ml/1 pint distilled malt vinegar
460g/1lb sugar
2 tbsps mustard seeds
½ tsp turmeric
1 tsp celery seeds
Pinch cayenne pepper

---

1. Slice the cucumbers and onion very thinly and place in a shallow dish.

2. Sprinkle liberally with salt, cover with a weighted lid and leave for at least 6 hours. Drain, rinse well in cold water and drain again.

3. Place the remaining ingredients in a large pan and bring to the boil, stirring well.

4. Boil for 2-3 minutes, add the sliced cucumber and onion.

5. Boil for 5 minutes or until the cucumber looks translucent.

6. Pour into hot, sterilized jars, then seal with acid-proof lids and label. Store refrigerated.

Corn Relish

MAKES About 1kg/2¼lbs

Popular for barbecues, this relish is delicious on sausages and hamburgers.

PREPARATION: 20 mins
COOKING: 35 mins

175g/6oz celery, chopped
1 onion, chopped
2 tsps celery seasoning
1 tsp mustard seed
¼ tsp turmeric
1 tbsp cornflour
340ml/12 fl oz distilled malt vinegar
200ml/7 fl oz water
340g/12oz sweetcorn niblets, fresh or frozen
2 red peppers, diced
120g/4oz sugar

---

1. Place the celery, onion, celery seasoning, mustard seeds, turmeric and cornflour in a large saucepan.

2. Gradually stir in the vinegar and water. Bring gently to the boil, stirring constantly, and cook for 5 minutes.

3. Stir in the sweetcorn, diced peppers and sugar and cook slowly for 25 minutes, stirring occasionally, until the mixture is very thick and the vegetables are tender. Test by stirring with a wooden spoon – if the spoon leaves a channel then the mixture is ready.

4. Pour into hot, sterilized jars, then seal and label.

Piccalilli

MAKES About 1kg/2¼lbs

A traditional English pickle. Any vegetables can be used, but this combination works well.

PREPARATION: 20 mins, plus 6 hrs standing
COOKING: 15-20 mins

340g/12oz pickling cucumbers, diced
340g/12oz onions, chopped
340g/12oz cauliflower, cut into small florets
1 large green pepper, diced
Salt
280ml/½ pint distilled malt vinegar
2 tbsps yellow mustard
½ tsp turmeric
½ tsp mustard seeds
¼ tsp dried thyme
1 bay leaf
60g/2oz sugar
1 tbsp cornflour mixed with a little water

---

1. Layer the vegetables in a dish, sprinkle each layer liberally with salt.

2. Leave for at least 6 hours to draw out water from the vegetables. Rinse and drain well.

3. Place the vegetables in a large saucepan or preserving pan and add the vinegar, mustard, turmeric, mustard seeds, thyme, bay leaf and sugar.

4. Stir to mix well. Bring gently to the boil and simmer for 8 minutes, or until the vegetables are cooked but still crisp.

5. Stir in the cornflour mixture and cook until thickened.

6. Pour into hot, sterilized jars, then seal with acid-proof lids and label. Store refrigerated.

Sweet Pickled Onions

MAKES About 1.8kg/4lbs

*Nothing can compare with the flavour of home-made pickled onions,
perfect for picnics, salads or bread and cheese.*

PREPARATION: 20 mins
COOKING: 1 hr

1.4kg/3lbs button or pickling onions
850ml/1½ pints malt, distilled, or cider vinegar
340g/12oz light muscovado sugar
2 tbsps mustard seeds
1 cinnamon stick
1 tsp salt

1. Pour boiling water over the onions to loosen the skins, then peel them.

2. Bring a large pan of water to the boil, add a couple of tablespoons of the vinegar, add the onions and blanch for 5 minutes.

3. Drain the onions and pat dry, then pack tightly into heatproof preserving jars.

Step 1 Drain the blanched onions and peel off the skins.

Step 4 Pour the boiling vinegar over the onions to within 1cm/⅓-inch of the top of the jar.

4. Heat the remaining ingredients together until boiling and pour over the onions to within 1cm/⅓ inch of the top of the jar. Screw the lids onto the jars then release a quarter turn.

5. Place several layers of folded newspaper in the bottom of a pan which is deep enough to fill with water to the top of the jars. Place the jars in the pan.

6. Fill the pan with water up to the neck of the jars and heat slowly to simmering point, this should take about 30 minutes.

7. Maintain the water at simmering point for 10 minutes.

8. Turn off the heat, tighten the lids and allow the jars to cool completely in the water.

9. Label and store in a cool dark place.

Pumpkin Chutney

MAKES About 1.8kg/4lbs

A chunky pickle, delicious served with a ploughman's lunch.

PREPARATION: 20 mins
COOKING: 45 mins

1.4kg/3lbs pumpkin flesh, small diced
2 lemons, thinly sliced
2 tbsps grated fresh root ginger
340g/12oz raisins
700ml/1¼ pints water
570ml/1 pint white wine vinegar
900g/2lbs demerara sugar

1. Place all the ingredients except the sugar in a preserving pan. Cook gently for 20-30 minutes until the pumpkin is tender.

2. Stir in the sugar and heat gently until it is dissolved.

3. Turn up the heat and bring to the boil. Boil rapidly until thickened, stirring frequently to prevent it from burning on the bottom of the pan.

4. Test by stirring with a wooden spoon; if the spoon leaves a channel then the mixture is ready.

5. Pour into hot, sterilized jars, then seal and label.

Index